Mimi's Village

To Baird & Leah, who spend each day helping children to live, and live healthier — K.S.M.

For Katie — E.F.

CitizenKid™ is a trademark of Kids Can Press Ltd.

Text © 2012 Katie Smith Milway
Illustrations © 2012 Eugenie Fernandes

Kids Can Press acknowledges the financial support of the Government of Ontario, through the Ontario Media Development Corporation's Ontario Book Initiative; the Ontario Arts Council; the Canada Council for the Arts; and the Government of Canada, through the BPIDP, for our publishing activity.

Published in Canada by
Kids Can Press Ltd.
25 Dockside Drive
Toronto, ON M5A 0B5

Published in the U.S. by
Kids Can Press Ltd.
2250 Military Road
Tonawanda, NY 14150

www.kidscanpress.com

The artwork in this book was rendered in acrylic.
The text is set in Shannon Std.

Edited by Valerie Wyatt
Designed by Marie Bartholomew
Photos on pages 26 and 27: Michael Milway

This book is smyth sewn casebound.
Manufactured in China, in 3/2012, through
Asia Pacific Offset, 3/F, New factory (No.12),
Jing Yi Industrial Center, Tian Bei Estate, Fu Ming
Community, Guan Lan, Bao An, Shenzhen, China

FSC
www.fsc.org
MIX
Paper from
responsible sources
FSC® C012521

CM 12 0 9 8 7 6 5 4 3 2 1

Library and Archives Canada Cataloguing in Publication

Milway, Katie Smith, 1960–
    Mimi's village : and how basic health care transformed it / by Katie Smith Milway ; illustrated by Eugenie Fernandes.

ISBN 978-1-55453-722-8

1. Public health — Kenya — Juvenile fiction. 2. Medical care — Kenya — Juvenile fiction. 3. Nutrition — Kenya — Juvenile fiction. 4. Malaria — Kenya — Juvenile fiction. I. Fernandes, Eugenie, 1943– II. Title.

PS8626.I48M54 2012   jC813'.6   C2011-908483-X

Kids Can Press is a *l'orus*™ Entertainment company

Mimi's Village

And How Basic Health Care Transformed It

Written by Katie Smith Milway

Illustrated by Eugenie Fernandes

CitizenKid™

Kids Can Press

Sadness in the Village

Mimi Malaho says good-bye to her Ma and watches from the shadows as the mothers of the village gather. One of the village babies, little Kanzi, died in the night. Now the women will sit and weep with Kanzi's Ma, sharing food out of a common bowl.

Mimi is too young to join the women. As she walks slowly home, she smells the smoke from wood fires mixing with the earthy scent of the maize fields. The moon lights a path to the Malahos' home. Inside, her little sister, Nakkissi, is sleeping, while her brother, Wafula, is carving wood figures with Pa. So far, the Malahos have been lucky. No terrible sickness has come to their family.

Mimi thinks about her Ma, who will have another baby in a few months. She hopes the new baby will be healthy. But she knows there are many things in this part of Kenya that can take a child and carry her away.

5

Danger in the Water

The next day is hot and dry. It is Mimi and Nakkissi's job to fetch water. Mimi hoists a water can onto her shoulder and grabs Nakkissi's free hand. Nakkissi carries her own small can.

They wave as they pass by the maize fields where Pa and Wafula are weeding. It is so quiet they can hear the crickets hopping from stalk to stalk. As the girls enter the forest, birds flutter up to higher branches, and a small antelope, a tiny *dik-dik*, leaps for cover.

Nakkissi is named after the antelope, but today she is not leaping. She is hot and thirsty and dragging her feet. When they arrive at the stream, Nakkissi begs Mimi for water. Mimi knows the water has to be boiled before they can drink it to kill the bugs that carry sickness. And so she tells Nakkissi she must wait.

Halfway home, a snake slithers across their path. Nakkissi jumps and spills her can of water. Now they must return to the stream, and Mimi knows that Nakkissi will not make it home without a drink.

At the stream, she gives Nakkissi two handfuls of the brownish water, hoping a little won't hurt. "Do not tell Ma or Pa," she warns her little sister.

Sickness at Home

At dinner, Nakkissi eats only a few mouthfuls of *ugali*. As the sky darkens, the little girl becomes sick and throws up the bit she has eaten. Mimi knows she must confess. "I gave Nakkissi water from the stream today," she tells Ma and Pa. "She was so thirsty she would not walk."

"Mimi, you know better," says Pa. But he and Ma are too worried about Nakkissi to scold. There is no doctor or nurse in their village to call for help.

Ma gives Nakkissi water that has been boiled and cooled, but Nakkissi cannot keep it down. With nothing left in her tummy, she looks like a doll made of rags. Then she begins to moan. Mimi is afraid. Many children do not recover from such illness.

Ma and Pa know what they must do. They wrap Nakkissi in a blanket and put her in their cart. Pa takes his machete and Wafula grabs his hoe, while Ma and Mimi carry sticks in case they meet animals that prowl at night. They walk for an hour down the path that leads to the next village, keeping their ears and eyes open. But the only frightening sounds are Nakkissi's soft moans.

Finally, they arrive at the health clinic and lay out their blankets beside the other families who have come for help. They all must wait until the clinic opens the next morning.

Huddled in her mother's arms, Nakkissi closes her eyes and breathes weakly. Mimi falls asleep holding her sister's hand.

Simple Cures

In the morning, a tall woman with a big smile arrives at the clinic. It is Nurse Tela. She is gentle with Nakkissi and speaks firmly with her parents. "Your daughter has lost fluid. I will give her clean water mixed with a little sugar and salt."

Nurse Tela shows Ma how to make the mixture and use a dropper to give some to Nakkissi. "The sugar will give her energy, and the salt will help her body hold the water," Nurse Tela explains. Nakkissi will need a dropper of fluid every five minutes for the next few hours to regain strength.

Behind them, women are lining up with their babies. Mimi watches Nurse Tela weigh each baby and give the mother a vitamin to make her milk healthy.

She beckons to Mimi and asks her to keep the babies happy as she puts them on the scale. "Why do you weigh them?" Mimi asks shyly.

"So we can tell they are growing," says Nurse Tela, giving a fat baby back to her mother. "I see your family has a baby on the way, too," she says. "If your Ma feeds the new baby mother's milk for many months, it will grow and be healthy, too. You will see."

Mimi wonders if Nurse Tela could weigh their new baby when it comes.

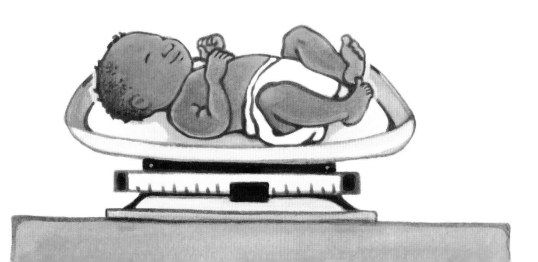

A Good Sign

The afternoon grows long, and Nurse Tela stops by each family one last time. She asks a little boy to stick out his tongue. She takes the pulse of another child. Finally, she checks on Nakkissi. She is doing better, but the nurse persuades the Malahos to keep the children at the clinic overnight. Tomorrow, she tells them, is vaccination day — if all three children stay, they can get their shots.

Ma and Pa decide that the children will stay with Ma, while Pa goes home to milk their goats. Mimi and Wafula walk their father to the edge of the forest. As they say good-bye, a big stork startles out of a tree, flapping its huge wings. Mimi remembers a story her Pa has told her about the stork that grants wishes when it flies. She closes her eyes and makes a wish.

That night, as Mimi and her family bed down, she hears chattering high up in the trees. It is a family of monkeys, a safe, familiar sound. Better yet, the sad moaning sound has gone. Nakkissi is fast asleep, breathing softly.

Vaccination Day

In the morning, Mimi and Wafula are first in line at the clinic, ready for their vaccinations. Nakkissi snuggles in Ma's arms. She is well enough to have her vaccination, too.

Behind the Malahos, there is a long line of parents with their children. Some have traveled many hours to be here. They know that vaccinations can keep the children from getting sick or even worse.

Mimi is afraid of the needle, but her mother puts a firm hand on her shoulder. Nurse Tela calls her name.

As Mimi steps forward, a young woman brushes past her. She is carrying a small boy who lies limp in her arms. Nurse Tela takes a look at the child and says one word: malaria. The mothers and fathers murmur and pass the news back down the line.

Everyone knows about malaria. It is a disease that can cause sickness and even death. It is carried by mosquitoes, and mosquitoes are everywhere in this part of the country. This little boy is lucky. His mother has brought him to the clinic in time. He will get medicine to make him better.

Nurse Tela talks to the mother and gives the boy a pill, then she turns back to Mimi. It is time for her vaccination. Mimi squeezes her eyes shut and counts in her head. It is all over before she gets to five. Wafula goes next, and he is very brave.

Pa arrives to take them home. He holds Mimi's hand and listens to her stories as they walk. Mimi talks excitedly about Nakkissi's recovery, the monkeys in the trees and their vaccinations (which didn't hurt so much). When she tells Pa about the boy with malaria, he falls silent.

■ ■ ■ ■ ■ ■ ■ ■ ■

A Big Dream

Over their evening meal, Pa tells Ma he is worried. The rainy season has begun and with it come the mosquitoes that bring malaria. They will have their new baby soon, as will other families in the village. The babies and children are at risk of malaria, pneumonia and other diseases. Ma says what they have all been thinking. "Our village needs a nurse and a clinic. But where will the money come from?"

Mimi lifts Nakkissi onto her lap. What would have happened to her without Nurse Tela? Mimi remembers seeing the stork and the wish she made — for a nurse of their own.

That night Mimi sleeps fitfully and dreams a giant mosquito is chasing her. Then a tall woman in white appears and shoos the monster away.

When Mimi awakes, she has an idea. She hears her father washing and joins him at the basin. "Pa, you and our uncles built our house, didn't you?" Pa nods. "Could you build a clinic, too? Maybe then a nurse would come." Her father says it is a good dream — but a big dream — and pats her on the head.

Pa leaves for the maize fields, but when he gets home that night he has changed his mind. Why not try it? He will talk to the elders of the village. If they can find materials, they can work together to build a clinic. And if each family puts aside a little bit of their maize profits, maybe they can hire a nurse.

A Clinic for Mimi's Village

It is three months later, and so much has happened.

The elders agreed with Mimi's idea. The mission church donated materials and a plot of land — a gift, they said, that came from friends living far away. Mimi's father and other men worked hard, after long days in the fields, to build a small, square structure with a strong tin roof. The door has a padlock to keep supplies safe and a big red cross.

Meanwhile, Mimi's Ma and other women in the village formed a health committee. Together, they visited the government office a half day's walk away to request medicines and a nurse. They showed the officer the maize money they had saved, and he agreed to send them what they needed.

Mimi looks at the neat rows of supplies. Her wish is coming true. Today, their nurse will make her first visit, and the village has planned a big celebration with roasted goat, yams and *irio*. When the nurse arrives, it is … Nurse Tela! Mimi runs to her calling out a welcome, "*Karibu, karibu!*"

The village women are wearing their best *kangas* and head scarves. Some men bring out goat-skin drums, and Pa strums a *litungu*. Mimi, Wafula and other children dance the *kamabeka*. They bob their heads and bodies back and forth as they hop from foot to foot.

Mimi will never forget this wonderful day. She looks over to catch her mother's eye. But her mother is distracted, sitting quietly under a tree and taking big breaths. Mimi goes to her. "The baby is coming …" gasps Ma, "… coming quickly."

□ □ □ □ □ □ □ □ □ □ □

A Healthy Birth

Mimi runs to Pa and Nurse Tela shouting, "The baby is coming!" Nurse Tela grabs her kit and tells Mimi to boil water.

"Bring a big bowl of it and clean blankets," she instructs. When Mimi returns, Nurse Tela washes her hands in the hot water.

Mimi, Wafula and Nakkissi hunker down on their knees outside the clinic. What is taking so long? Could something be wrong? Using sticks, they draw names for the new baby in the dirt — perhaps W-E-K-E-S-A for a boy born at harvest time? Or N-E-K-E-S-A for a girl? Then, after even more time, they hear a cry.

Pa comes out with a big smile on his face. "It is a boy!" he shouts. Mimi squeezes past him and watches as Nurse Tela dries the baby off and wraps him in a clean blanket. Pa holds up the little boy for all to see. "Meet our new son," says Pa. "We will call him Jomo, after our country's first president." Everyone cheers, but the loudest cheers come from Mimi, Wafula and Nakkissi.

Jomo has had a good start. He is the clinic's first baby, but he will not be its last.

Healthy Habits

The next time Nurse Tela visits Mimi's village, she weighs little Jomo and the other babies, while Mimi keeps them happy.

Mimi looks forward to Nurse Tela's visits. Each time, the nurse has a new surprise.

One week, she shows families how to wash their vegetables and fruit in water mixed with a little bleach to kill the bugs. A drop of the same bleach in their drinking water will make it safe, too, she tells them.

Another week, Nurse Tela brings a new recipe for *ugali*. This version adds vegetables to the maize porridge. Better food, she says, will make their bodies stronger so they can fight off sickness.

But the nets are the biggest surprise of all. Mimi thinks they are wonderful. She could wear one as a fancy *kitenge*, or Wafula could use one to catch tilapia so they can make fish stew.

But Nurse Tela explains that the nets are sprayed with insect killer and are to be used to protect the villagers from mosquitoes and the malaria they carry. "You drape the net over your mattress and sleep underneath it," she says. "It will keep mosquitoes away at night and kill any that land. If the mosquitoes can't bite, they will have no food and will die away."

Mimi tries her new net that night, with Nakkissi sleeping close beside her. Now and then she hears the whine of a mosquito, but beneath her net, she feels safe and sound.

□ □ □ □ □ □ □ □ □ □ □ □

A Healthy Village

Jomo and the clinic are now one year old. To mark the day, Mimi and Ma join the village health committee. They sing and clap and share a bowl of roasted crickets.

So much has changed since Nakkissi's illness. There is still sickness from time to time in the village, but the Malahos and the other families fear it less. They can prevent many illnesses now, and when someone does become sick, they have medicines and a nurse to help.

Nurse Tela still comes every two weeks. But now she is training Ma to deliver babies and other mothers to weigh them and give out medicines when she cannot be there.

Mimi watches and listens as Nurse Tela talks to the village women. Her wish for a clinic came true. Now she is starting to dream a much bigger dream — that one day, perhaps she can become a nurse or a doctor and help other villages become healthy, too.

A Real Village Health Worker

The story of Mimi and Nurse Tela is based on a blend of real stories. One is taking place today in Zambia in southern Africa, where Joyce Siakalebonene, a 43-year-old widow, lives in a compound bustling with ducks, chickens, goats and children. The family is healthy today, thanks to help from an international aid organization, a village health worker and their own actions.

In front of Joyce's compound is the village well that was built with help from the aid organization World Vision and contributions from the village. Joyce's only water source used to be a polluted water hole shared with animals. The water often made her family ill. The new well provides clean water for cooking and cleaning. Behind Joyce's two-room brick house, she has built a latrine (toilet) and a simple washbasin, which

is just a water-filled jug with a hole in the bottom plugged with a stick. To "turn on the faucet," Joyce pulls out the stick. The simple act of washing hands before eating has reduced diseases in the family.

Another health problem comes with mosquitoes, some of which carry malaria from one person to another, infecting them when they bite. Joyce's husband died from malaria. Fortunately, by the time her daughter, Beauty, contracted malaria, the village had a health worker, Felina Maiya. Felina brought Beauty medicine, and then made sure she got to a clinic for more treatment.

Felina lives near Joyce. Her compound is spic and span. Her bedroom has a large, insecticide-treated bed net draped over her mattress. Outside, the shrubs have been cut back to keep mosquitoes away.

Beauty Siakalebonene, 8, in pink dress, at her community's new well. Beauty recovered from malaria with help from her village health care volunteer.

Rachel and William Falb (left and center) of Wellesley, Massachusetts, pack health care kits at Boston AIDS Africa. World Vision distributes the kits to volunteer health care workers like Felina Maiya.

In addition to running her own busy household, Felina voluntarily cares for neighboring families with orphans or vulnerable children. She checks in on each family, providing help with simple treatments, such as aspirin and oral rehydration, a solution of a sweetened liquid and salt, for dehydration. She encourages children with the disease HIV to take their medicine. She identifies those that she cannot treat and urges them to go to a clinic. Since beginning her work in 2006, she has monitored sixty-one households.

World Vision provides Felina with a bicycle, ongoing training and a kit full of medical supplies donated by health care organizations and assembled by volunteers in Boston, Massachusetts.

Recently, Felina was asked to take on an additional job — that of hygiene promoter. She encourages people to set up drying racks for their dishes to keep the dishes away from germs and to build latrines for sanitation. "I also educate the community to wash their hands with soap before they touch or prepare food," she says, "and to cover their water and add chlorine to purify it. If they don't have chlorine, they have to boil their water." Felina is working to prevent diseases such as diarrhea and dysentery that are killers of children under five.

She also works to prevent malaria, called *tutamanzi* in her local language. "The carrier mosquitoes bite between 10 p.m. and 4 a.m., so everyone should use a bed net every night," Felina explains to one family, the Wilsons. She unwraps a treated net from its package. Then she asks if she can show the family how to hang the net over the bed. Mr. Wilson nods and his family of ten watches how it is done. If they follow Felina's instructions, the Wilsons will have a much better chance of staying healthy.

Felina cares about her community and the health of its families, particularly the children. "I have seen the orphaned children. When they don't have anyone to love them, they get depressed and lose hope. I feel I can bring them and their guardians encouragement and love." She also feels that she is saving lives. "In the past, people used to die because of diarrhea and malaria, so I wanted to help change this. I feel I really am changing attitudes."

Felina Maiya, the health care volunteer, bicycles to neighboring families to distribute bed nets.

Felina demonstrates a bed net at the Wilson family's home.

Why Is Basic Health Care So Important?

Nurse Tela and the real-life Felina are providing basic health care. This care includes educating people to prevent the spread of diseases and providing simple cures for common, treatable illnesses, such as dehydration. Most importantly, people are taught what to eat and drink and how to live so they stay healthy.

Basic health care can make a big difference in poor countries, where illnesses that are considered minor or even non-existent in other nations are some of the biggest killers. Today, according to the World Health Organization:

- Diarrhea causes one in five deaths around the world.
- Pneumonia causes two million deaths a year.
- Malaria kills one child in sub-Saharan Africa every 45 seconds.

Even diseases such as tuberculosis, measles and smallpox, which have been stamped out by vaccinations in many countries, continue to take lives in Africa and other parts of the developing world. And now AIDS, a disease that develops from a virus called HIV, has become one of the most deadly diseases in developing countries. Kanzi's death at the beginning of this book could have been caused by any of these diseases. In fact, every day, on average, 21 000 children under the age of five die, most of them from diseases that could have been prevented with basic health care.

According to the United Nations Children's Fund (UNICEF), there are four main threats to children's health in the developing world:

1. Lack of adequate food
2. Diseases such as pneumonia, malaria, tuberculosis and AIDS
3. Lack of safe drinking water and basic sanitation, which can lead to diarrhea-related diseases
4. Poor health care of mothers, which often results in the poor health of their babies

But if a child can live past age five, the chance of her survival, even in countries with poor health care, dramatically increases.

To promote survival, health workers from nonprofit groups, government agencies and international organizations, such as UNICEF, recommend the following measures:

1. Vitamin A supplements and breastfeeding for infants up to six months old to improve nutrition in babies and children
2. Disease prevention, including:
   - Affordable vaccinations, immunizations and antibiotics to prevent or treat childhood diseases, such as pneumonia and measles
   - Treatment with drugs to protect children from developing AIDS and to help prevent the spread of the disease from mothers to their babies
   - Nets treated with insecticide to shield children from the mosquitoes that cause malaria
3. Safe drinking water and basic sanitation facilities, such as latrines, to help children avoid diarrhea
4. Care before, during and after childbirth by a health worker to improve the health and lives of newborns and mothers

The **health clinic** organizes vaccinations, dispenses medicine and helps mothers prepare for their babies, deliver them and keep them safe.

At **school** children learn many things, including healthy habits.

A **latrine** improves sanitation, which can prevent illnesses such as diarrhea.

A **well** provides clean water for washing hands and bodies and safe water for drinking. This improves hygiene and stops many diseases.

A **bed net** sprayed with insecticide keeps out the mosquitoes that carry malaria.

Growing fresh vegetables adds vitamins to families' main diet of maize, which improves nutrition.

Boiling water kills bacteria that can cause diarrhea or vomiting.

How Can You Help?

Have you ever thought that the money you earn doing chores or selling lemonade and cookies could actually save a life? Well, it could. And if you think big, you could save many lives. For example, in 2004, a nine-year-old boy in Arizona named Austin Gutwein organized a basketball shoot-a-thon called Hoops of Hope to help AIDS orphans. Since then, more than 25 000 kids have participated in Hoops of Hope events. They've raised $2.5 million, which has funded the construction of a high school and AIDS clinics in Zambia, bought 750 mosquito nets and financed much more. In Ontario, seven-year-old Ryan Hreljac raised money to build a well in Uganda in 1999. He went on to found Ryan's Well Foundation, which has since funded more than 1500 well and sanitation projects in 16 countries.

Here are some ways *you* can put *your* allowance or earnings to work to help those less fortunate lead healthier lives (2012 prices):

- $8 provides 100 packets of special powder that, when mixed with water, can save a child from deadly dehydration. See http://youth.unicefusa.org/assets/pdf/tot-resource-center-/2010-tot-what-your-money-can-buy.pdf.
- $18 buys three bed nets for a family to prevent malaria. See www.netsforlifeafrica.org or World Vision's www.endmalaria.org.
- $25 gets the word out to African families about malaria prevention. See www.malarianomore.org.
- $50 pays to ship $550 worth of donated medicines to health clinics overseas. See the gift catalog at www.worldvision.org.
- $70 buys high protein food to treat malnourished children. See the gift catalog at www.savethechildren.org.
- $100 pays for a share of a well supplying clean water. See www.ryanswell.ca.
- $240 pays for two families to receive farm tools, seed and fertilizer in Western Kenya. See www.oneacrefund.org.
- $250 is the fundraising goal for joining a Hoops of Hope basketball shoot-a-thon to raise money to help AIDS orphans in Africa. See www.hoopsofhope.org.

Here is Ryan Hreljac in Uganda, where he went to see the well he had built.

Austin Gutwein (left), founder of Hoops of Hope, with Samuel, an AIDS patient, in Rwanda.

Building a healthy village is a process that takes many years and requires the help of many organizations and individuals, including you. Clean water and the means to grow or buy enough food is the foundation. Access to basic health care is the next step. Then comes literacy, which gives families like the Malahos the chance to learn more about health and nutrition. Schooling is also vital because it encourages children like Mimi, Wafula, Nakkissi and Jomo to follow their dreams and become health workers, water or farm specialists, teachers and more. Over time, with the help of people locally and globally, villages can move from basic health to prosperity.

Bed nets prevent malaria-carrying mosquitoes from infecting sleepers. Without victims, the carrier mosquitoes die off.

New Ways to Create Change

Quality Care for All

Partners In Health (PIH) is dedicated to providing high-quality health care to poor people in 12 countries around the world. PIH does whatever it takes to get patients the care they need. Community health workers visit patients in their homes, making sure sick people get to see a doctor. The health workers are also trained to notice when a family does not have enough food or their roof is leaking. Then PIH works to fix these problems as well. For example, when PIH's team in Haiti found a child who was severely malnourished, they treated the child with a high-calorie, peanut butter–based food called Nourimanba. This was an easy and fast treatment the family could continue at home. But PIH didn't stop there. The family was connected with a community agriculture worker, who helped them improve their farming methods to grow more crops so that no one went hungry. You can watch Partners In Health videos at www.youtube.com/partnersinhealth and share what you've learned with your friends and school.

Powerful Messages and Messengers

Malaria No More helps send bed nets to Africa and, with the help of celebrities, spreads the word about malaria prevention and how bed nets can help. For example, Africa's most famous musician, Youssou N'Dour, uses his concerts to urge African families to sleep under their bed nets and seek treatment for malaria. Malaria No More also uses African TV and radio and text messages to reach families with nightly reminders to use their bed nets. Getting the word out like this is called "advocacy" and kids can do it, too. How could you get the word out on healthy habits, such as always sneezing or coughing into your elbow, not your hand? Read more about Malaria No More and its Africa programs at www.malarianomore.org.

Stopping Disease

North America and Europe suffered from malaria until the mid-1900s when an insecticide campaign wiped out the Anopheles mosquito that carries the disease. In 2007, the Bill & Melinda Gates Foundation began calling for a similar campaign in parts of Africa, Asia and Latin America to eliminate malaria. The foundation contributed $100 million per year for five years to The Global Fund to Fight AIDS, Tuberculosis and Malaria. The World Health Organization took up the challenge and increased funding for prevention. As a result, rates of malaria are now falling. Bed nets and other prevention techniques work, and they cost no more than $10. If every child in North America and Europe funded one bed net for Africa, we'd be well on our way to stamping out malaria. For more information, go to www.mimisvillage.org.

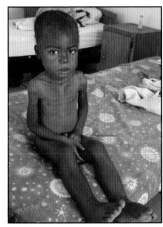 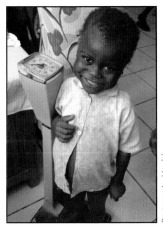

Partners In Health

Haitian youngster Jean-Luc before and after his Nourimanba treatment for severe malnourishment.

Malaria No More

African superstar Youssou N'Dour of Senegal puts on Xeex Sibbiru (Fight Malaria) concerts to urge fans to use bed nets.

☐ ☐ ☐ ☐ ☐ ☐ ☐ ☐ ☐ ☐ ☐
Glossary

Mimi's Village is set in Bungoma, Western Kenya, where locals speak both Swahili and Luyha dialects, such as Bukusu.

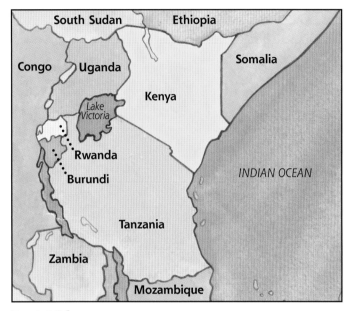

East Africa

dik-dik: a very small antelope, standing just 30 cm (1 ft.) high at the shoulder

irio: a dish made of mashed potatoes, peas and corn

Jomo: the first name of Jomo Kenyatta (1894–1978), Kenya's father of independence and first president

kamabeka: a dance common to the Bungoma region

kanga: the Swahili word for a cloth wrap that has a border along all four sides

karibu: the Swahili word for "welcome"

kitenge: the Swahili word for a cloth wrap similar to the *kanga*, but with a border on only one side

litungu: a harp-like instrument native to Western Kenya

machete: a broad, heavy, all-purpose knife used to cut grasses and shrubs, slaughter animals and defend people

maize: a type of corn

malaria: a fever caused by a parasite that is carried by female Anopheles mosquitoes

Mimi: in Swahili or Bukusu *mimi* means "I am"

Nakkissi: a girl born in sight of an antelope

Nekesa: the Bukusu name for a girl born during the harvest

oral rehydration: usually a mixture of sweetened water or juice and some salt that allows the body to hold water

pneumonia: a disease that inflames the lungs

tilapia: a common white fish in Lake Victoria

ugali: maize porridge

vaccination: a shot to stimulate the body's immune system to fight a particular disease

Wafula: a boy born in sight of a baboon

Wekesa: the Bukusu name for a boy born at harvest